Dear Parent:

Your child's love of reading starts here!

Every child learns to read in a different way and at his or her own speed. Some go back and forth between reading levels and read favorite books again and again. Others read through each level in order. You can help your young reader improve and become more confident by encouraging his or her own interests and abilities. From books your child reads with you to the first books he or she reads alone, there are I Can Read Books for every stage of reading:

SHARED READING
Basic language, word repetition, and whimsical illustrations, ideal for sharing with your emergent reader

BEGINNING READING
Short sentences, familiar words, and simple concepts for children eager to read on their own

READING WITH HELP
Engaging stories, longer sentences, and language play for developing readers

READING ALONE
Complex plots, challenging vocabulary, and high-interest topics for the independent reader

I Can Read Books have introduced children to the joy of reading since 1957. Featuring award-winning authors and illustrators and a fabulous cast of beloved characters, I Can Read Books set the standard for beginning readers.

A lifetime of discovery begins with the magical words **"I Can Read!"**

Visit www.icanread.com for information on enriching your child's reading experience.

Visit www.zonderkidz.com/icanread for more faith-based I Can Read! titles from Zonderkidz.

I'll go to the king. I'll do it even though it's against the law. And if I have to die, I'll die.
—*Esther 4:16*

ZONDERKIDZ

Brave Queen Esther

An **I Can Read Book**

Requests for information should be addressed to:
Zonderkidz, *3900 Sparks Drive SE, Grand Rapids, Michigan 49546*

Library of Congress Cataloging-in-Publication Data
Brave Queen Esther / illustrated by David Miles.
pages cm. – (Adventure Bible I can read ; Level 2)
Summary: "Written in the I can read level two standards, young readers learn about a young Jewish woman who is chosen to be a queen by a powerful king" – Provided by publisher.
Audiences: Ages 4-8.
ISBN 978-0-310-74666-9 (softcover) – ISBN 0-310-74666-3 (softcover) – ISBN 978-0-310-74652-2 (epub) – ISBN 978-0-310-74768-0 (epub) – ISBN 978-0-310-74771-0 (epub)
1. Esther, Queen of Persia–Juvenile literature. 2. Bible stories, English–Esther–Juvenile literature. I. Miles, David, 1973- illustrator.
BS580.E8B72 2015
222.909505–dc23 2014031548

Written by Breanna Dey
Editor: Mary Hassinger
Art direction and design: Kris Nelson

Printed in China

19 20 21 22 23 24 /DSC / 21 20 19 18 17 16 15 14 13 12 11 10 9 8 7 6 5

Adventure Bible

Brave Queen Esther

Pictures by David Miles

ZONDERkidz

Once there was a woman
named Esther.
She lived with her cousin Mordecai.

Mordecai took care of Esther.

Esther and Mordecai were Jewish.

Together they loved and worshipped God.

One day the king of the land
decided to look for a queen.
“We will find you a queen,”
said the men who helped him.

The men looked all over for a new queen.

Soon they saw Esther.

“We must take her

to the king,” they said.

The men brought Esther

to the palace.

The king thought Esther was

the most beautiful woman of all.

"I want you to be my queen,"

said the king.

Esther said, "Yes."

There was a great celebration.

Esther was happy.
She lived in the palace.
Esther's cousin, Mordecai,
worked in the palace.
Mordecai told Esther
to keep her faith a secret.
So Esther did not tell anyone
she and Mordecai were Jewish.

There was another man who worked in the palace.
His name was Haman.
He helped the king.

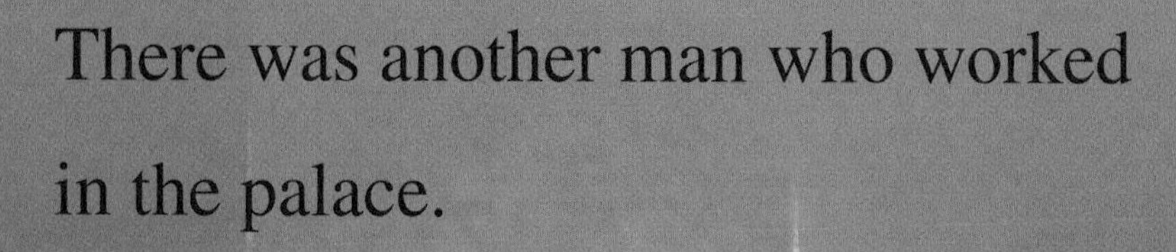

But he hated Mordecai and wanted
to be rid of all the Jews.
Haman spoke to the king,
"The Jews are bad! We don't need them
in our kingdom."

The king trusted Haman.
He agreed to get rid of the Jews.
Mordecai heard about Haman's plan.
He went to warn Esther
and see if she would help.

Mordecai said, “Esther, you must stop the king from harming us!”

“If I go to him,” Queen Esther said,
“I will get in trouble.
It is against the rules.”
But Mordecai knew Esther
was the only one who could help.

“Maybe God has made you queen

so you could save the Jews,”

Mordecai said.

Esther was afraid.

She knew if she went to the

king she would be in danger.

But Esther also knew God

would want her to be brave.

She prayed for courage.

Soon Esther went to the king.

She was still scared.

But the king was happy to see Esther.
He did not punish her
for coming to him.

So Esther invited the king
and Haman to a special dinner.
"I will give you a fine feast
if it pleases you,"
Queen Esther said.
The king was happy and told her
they would be there.

Esther made a delicious meal.
Esther, the king, and Haman
sat together and ate.
Then the king asked,
“What do you want, my queen?
You can have anything.”

Esther found the courage to speak.
“Please spare the Jews.
They are my people,” she said.
“Mordecai told me you have been
tricked, my king.”

“Tricked? By whom?” roared the king.

“Evil Haman,” Esther said.

The king was angry.

"Take Haman and arrest him!"

he yelled to his guards.

"Punish him for the

bad things he has done."

Now, the king gave Mordecai
an important job in the palace.
"You are a good man, Mordecai,"
said the king. "I will trust you
more than anyone else."

All the Jews were finally safe.

God had protected them,

with the help of Mordecai and Esther.

Esther helped save the Jews
by being brave and speaking up
for God's people.
She and her cousin Mordecai
were heroes.

“Hooray!” cried the Jews.

It was a time of happiness and joy

because of brave Queen Esther.

People of the Bible

Who knows but that you have come to your royal position for such a time as this?
—Esther 4:14

Esther

Esther was a young Jewish woman who lived in Persia. She became the queen of King Xerxes. When an evil man planned to kill all of the Jewish people in the land, Esther prayed to God for courage to help God's people.

Mordecai

Mordecai was a Jewish man. He had a niece named Esther. When her parents died, Mordecai adopted Esther to be his daughter and loved and cared for her. He helped Esther remember that she could be very brave, with God's help.

Did You Know?

The festival of Purim is celebrated by Jews every year. It is a reminder of when the Jewish people were saved from the evil plan of a man named Haman, in Persia long ago. Jewish people celebrate by having parties, eating good food, giving gifts of food, and also giving to charities.

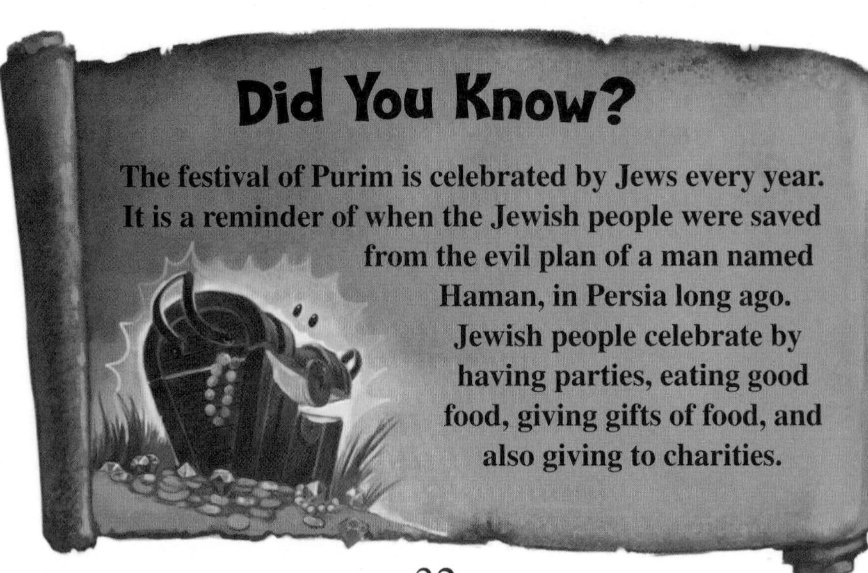